D1233177

Careers in Medical Technology

Bradley Steffens

ReferencePoint Press®

About the Author
Bradley Steffens is an award-winning poet, playwright, novelist, and author of more than thirty nonfiction books for children and young adults. He is a two-time recipient of the San Diego Book Award for Best Young Adult and Children's Nonfiction: His *Giants* won the 2005 award, and his *J.K. Rowling* claimed the 2007 prize. Steffens also received the Theodor S. Geisel Award for best book by a San Diego County author in 2007.

For more information, contact:
ReferencePoint Press, Inc.
PO Box 27779
San Diego, CA 92198
www.ReferencePointPress.com

Picture Credits:
Cover: Shutterstock.com/Darren Baker
 6: Maury Aaseng
19: iStockphoto/kali9
35: Shutterstock.com/Master Video
43: Thinkstock Images/iStock
52: Shutterstock.com/StockLite

LIBRARY OF CONGRESS CATALOGING-IN-PUBLICATION DATA

Name: Steffens, Bradley, 1955–
Title: Careers in medical technology / by Bradley Steffens.
Description: San Diego, CA : ReferencePoint Press, Inc., [2017] | Series: High-tech careers | Audience: Grade 9 to 12. | Includes bibliographical references and index.
Identifiers: LCCN 2016042050 (print) | LCCN 2016045642 (ebook) | ISBN 9781682821169 (hardback) | ISBN 9781682821176 (eBook)
Subjects: LCSH: Medical technology--Vocational guidance--Juvenile literature. | Medical technologists--Juvenile literature.
Classification: LCC R855.4 .S74 2017 (print) | LCC R855.4 (ebook) | DDC 610.28023--dc23
LC record available at https://lccn.loc.gov/2016042050

Contents

A Rewarding Career in a Resilient Industry

Technology is revolutionizing the practice of medicine. Whereas doctors once had to rely on two-dimensional X-rays and sonograms to see inside a patient's body, they now have high-definition, 3-D computer tomography that shows a patient's internal organs functioning in real time. Surgeons, who once had to perform operations by hand using powerful magnifying lenses, can now use tiny robotic arms the size of drinking straws and high-magnification cameras to operate deep inside the body with less bleeding and greater precision. Technology is also expanding available treatments and therapies. Once the only option for a patient with a malfunctioning organ was to receive an organ transplant, but now patients increasingly have the choice of receiving artificial organs made of materials less likely to be rejected by the body's immune system. Furthermore, the method of administering drugs and other treatments in a one-size-fits-all fashion is becoming obsolete. Using computer-assisted analysis, health care workers now stand on the threshold of being able to tailor therapies to individual patients based on their genetic code and the molecular interactions inside their cells. Technology is helping doctors deliver the right treatment that a specific patient needs to live a better life.

Technological advances and other factors, such as the general aging of the US population, have caused the health care sector of the American economy to grow at a much faster rate than the economy as a whole. According to the Bureau of Economic Analysis, the US economy grew at a rate of 0.8 percent in the first quarter of 2016, while the health care sector grew at a rate of 3.8 percent—nearly five times faster than the economy overall. The Office of the Actuary of the Centers for Medicare & Medicaid Services, a bureau within the Department of Health and Human Services, forecasts that expenditures on health care services will grow at an average rate of 5.8 percent per year between 2015 and 2025, about 1.3 percent higher than projected annual growth in the US gross domestic product. By 2025, health care spending will comprise 20.1 percent of the US economy, up from 17.5 percent in 2014. In 2015, the last year for which figures were available, annual health care expenditures surpassed $3 trillion for the first time.

Increased spending means an increased demand for services, and an increased demand for people to provide those services. According to the Bureau of Labor Statistics (BLS), a bureau within the Department of Labor, 20 million people were employed in health care occupations in 2014, accounting for more than 13 percent of the total US workforce. The growth in the health care sector has been phenomenal. Between 2004 and 2014, employment in health care occupations grew by more than 20 percent, while employment in all other occupations grew by only 3 percent during the same time period. The BLS projects continued growth. The bureau estimates that health care occupations will grow 19 percent from 2014 to 2024—almost three times faster than all occupations, which is projected at 7 percent. In fact, health care support occupations and health care practitioners and technical occupations are projected to be the two fastest-growing occupational groups from 2014 to 2024. Health care occupations are projected to contribute more new jobs to the economy than any other group, with a combined increase of 2.3 million jobs. Nearly one in four of all new jobs will be in the health care industry.

The projected growth for medical technology jobs is even faster than health care jobs as a whole. For example, the BLS projects the growth in the employment of diagnostic medical sonographers—medical technicians who take sonographic images of patients for use in medical diagnosis—to be about 26 percent from 2014 to 2024. The increasing demand for highly skilled medical professionals is outstripping the supply of qualified people to fill those positions. For example, the nation's medical labs need to fill more than seven thousand jobs each year, but US clinical laboratory education programs are producing only about six thousand new laboratory professionals each year, according to the National Accrediting Agency for Clinical Laboratory Sciences, leaving a gap of about 16 percent. The gap is even greater for physicians and surgeons. According to a 2016 study

Careers in Medical Tech

Occupation	Entry-Level Education	2015 Median Pay
Biochemist and biophysicist	Doctoral or professional degree	$82,150
Biological technician	Bachelor's degree	$41,650
Biomedical engineer	Bachelor's degree	$86,220
Chemist and materials scientist	Bachelor's degree	$72,610
Diagnostic medical sonographer, cardiovascular technologist and technician, including vascular technologist	Associate's degree	$63,630
EMT and paramedic	Postsecondary educational program	$31,980
Medical and clinical laboratory technologist and technician	Postsecondary certificate	$50,550
Medical scientist	Doctoral or professional degree	$82,240
Dispensing optician	High school diploma or equivalent	$34,840
Radiation therapist	Associate's degree	$80,220
Radiologic and MRI technologist	Associate's degree	$58,120
Statistician	Master's degree	$80,110
Veterinary technologist and technician	Associate's degree	$31,800

Source: Bureau of Labor Statistics, *Occupational Outlook Handbook*. www.bls.gov/ooh.

by the Conference Board, a nonprofit business research group organization, there are 17 percent more openings for physicians and surgeons than there are qualified professionals to fill them. The shortage in qualified Americans to fill these jobs has caused medical recruitment agencies to look for skilled workers overseas. In addition, many foreign-born students come to the United States to attend medical school or do graduate work in the life sciences. According to the Conference Board, 27 percent of all physicians practicing in the United States are immigrants.

A shortage of skilled workers means those candidates who can meet the requirements are in a position to command a higher salary. According to the BLS, in May 2015 the median annual wage for health care practitioners and technical occupations was $62,610, which was 72 percent higher than the median annual wage for all occupations ($36,200). People who pursue careers in medical technology are virtually guaranteed a well-paying, recession-proof career. In addition, they have the added reward of knowing they are spending their careers helping the healthy to avoid sickness, the sick to regain their health, the injured to heal, and those in pain to find relief.

Medical Research Scientist

What Does a Medical Research Scientist Do?

Medical research scientists drive biomedical research, discovering the causes of human diseases and identifying methods of preventing and treating them. The research they conduct, often called basic research, leads to a greater understanding of the underlying principles and mechanisms that affect health—all the way down to the molecular level. "Basic research forms the foundation for any translational research through which new methods for disease diagnosis, prevention and treatment are developed," Julie Decock, a cancer researcher at Qatar Biomedical Research Institute, Hamad bin Khalifa University in Doha, Qatar, told the author of this book. She added:

> To understand how you can prevent or fight a disease, you need to understand the basic mechanics. Gaining insight into the very basics of human biology is like finding this one

---

At a Glance:

Medical Research Scientist

Minimum Educational Requirements
PhD

Personal Qualities
Strong critical-thinking skills; detail oriented; passionate about science

Certification and Licensing
Medical licensing required when working with patients

Working Conditions
Indoors

Salary Range
About $44,500 to $155,000

Number of Jobs
About 108,000

Future Job Outlook
Growth of 8 percent by 2025

jigsaw piece which makes the other pieces of the puzzle fall into place. I have always been intrigued by what drives a cell to become malignant and grow into a tumor, and how these cells become so powerful that they can control someone's health. Cancer cells to me are like living organisms, they are very clever and often are one step ahead of us, escaping elimination by our immune system and resisting cancer treatment. Trying to understand how cancer cells outsmart us is what drives me in my quest to study and fight cancer.

The type of research a medical research scientist pursues often depends on where he or she works. Medical research scientists who work at colleges, universities, and government-sponsored laboratories often enjoy the freedom to pursue their research interests within the overall framework of the institution. Those who work in private industry usually conduct research aimed at achieving the goals of the company, whether it matches their personal interests or not.

Medical research scientists engaged in basic and translational research at universities and government laboratories most often secure funding by writing proposals to grant-funding institutions, such as government agencies, private funding sources, and charities. Researchers linked to a university will often be professors and have teaching responsibilities. Those who work in private industry are usually well funded, but they often have to discuss their research with nonscientist executives within the context of a business model.

The main output of a medical research scientist is a research paper published in a peer-reviewed journal. Medical research scientists gain prestige and recognition in the field by improving their scholarly rating, as measured by the Hirsch index, or h-index. The h-index measures both how often a scientist publishes new work as well as the impact of that research, based on the number of times the work is cited by other scientists. The more recognition a researcher receives, the more other researchers are interested in conducting collaborative research, the more high-quality results can be obtained, and the more papers can be published, resulting in more recognition and funding.

Medical research scientists often specialize in one area of research for their whole career. For example, cancer researchers investigate the causes of cancer as well as measures to prevent and treat the disease. Immunologists study the activation and function of the immune system in the defense against diseases. Gerontologists study the biology of aging, investigating why people develop various conditions in their later years and looking for ways to reverse or slow the onset of such conditions. Immunochemists investigate the interaction between various chemicals and the immune system. Serologists study fluids found in the human body, often concentrating on antibodies, proteins, and other chemicals found in blood serum. Toxicologists investigate the harmful effects various substances, such as chemicals and poisons, can have on human health.

One of the newest branches of biomedical research is known as systems biology. Systems biologists study entire systems of biological components—such as genes, molecules, cells, organisms, or entire species—rather than individual parts. Systems biologists measure the behavior of interacting components, using systematic technologies such as genomics, proteomics, and mathematical and computational models to describe and predict the behavior of systems.

How Do You Become a Medical Research Scientist?

Education

The majority of medical research scientists have a PhD in biology or a related life science, although a small percentage are medical doctors, holding an MD degree. Some medical research scientists pursue dual degrees, focusing on research methods in their PhD work and learning clinical skills for an MD degree.

Students who want to become medical research scientists usually obtain a bachelor's or a master's degree in biology or a related field. After graduation, they secure a position in a laboratory that has funding to host them so they can enter a PhD program to learn how to independently perform and interpret laboratory work. A PhD program culminates in the writing of a thesis that the candidate presents before a committee of professors. The majority of PhD programs requires the candidate to publish at least one scientific paper in a peer-reviewed journal.

Certification and Licensing

Medical research scientists who are engaged in research normally do not need licenses or certifications, except for those who conduct research using animals or are involved in clinical research. Scientists who administer investigational drugs or treatments—such as gene therapy or stem cell therapy—need to have a medical license or collaborate with someone who does.

Volunteer Work and Internships

Because of the high cost of the advanced materials and equipment needed to outfit a medical research laboratory, only well-funded organizations conduct medical research, and they do not seek volunteer assistance. However, some organizations offer internships to promising students. For example, the National Institutes of Health, an agency of the US government, offers a summer internship program with more than eleven hundred openings for high school, undergraduate, and graduate students. Many colleges and universities offer internships as well.

Skills and Personality

Successful medical research scientists have excellent observational skills. Whether working with biological samples or computer data, medical research scientists must make precise observations. Anything less can lead to inconclusive or incorrect results, sending the scientist down the wrong path.

A closely related skill is the ability to critically analyze data. This means looking at test results not only carefully but also objectively. The medical research scientist must guard against hoping for a certain outcome to prove a hypothesis correct or incorrect. The medical research scientist must weigh all of the information fairly without prejudice and remain open minded about any possible outcome.

A medical research scientist must have good communication skills. Scientists often work in teams of several collaborators, often located around the world. Communication is vital to the success of such collaborations. Scientists must also communicate with the research assistants, laboratory technicians, and other staff so the experiments are performed correctly. Scientists must be able to explain their research in publications, the media, and in research proposals—either to their employers or to grant-making organizations. "Foremost, a researcher needs to be passionate about what he or she does and not easily be discouraged," says Dr. Decock. "Medical research involves the study of very complex systems such as the human body, and very often things don't go as planned or expected. In research, the majority of your work will fail, but the few successes are what drives a researcher. If you are not passionate about what you do, you will not be able to handle the disappointment when another failure comes around."

On the Job

Employers

Medical research scientists work for a variety of employers. About one-third (34 percent) work in research and development for private companies and government laboratories. About 27 percent work at public and private colleges, universities, and professional schools. Some public and private hospitals conduct clinical research, employing about 15 percent of medical research scientists. Pharmaceutical companies and medical device manufacturers employ about 6 percent of medical research scientists. Medical and diagnostic laboratories employ about 4 percent, and the rest work for medical supply companies, patent offices, and elsewhere.

Working Conditions

Medical research scientists usually spend part of their time working in laboratories and the rest of their time working in offices. Early in their careers, scientists may spend a great deal of time in the laboratory; but once they are established, they spend the majority of time in their offices, keeping up with the literature in their field, studying the data from their own research, and writing research papers. Medical research scientists sometimes work with dangerous chemicals and biological samples and must take care to follow appropriate safety procedures.

Earnings

According to the Bureau of Labor Statistics, the median annual wage for medical research scientists was $82,240 in May 2015. The lowest 10 percent earned less than $44,510, and the highest 10 percent earned more than $155,000. Salaries of medical research scientists vary greatly, depending on the industry in which they are employed. For example, the median annual salary of scientists working in pharmaceutical and medicine manufacturing is $108,200, while the median in colleges, universities, and professional schools is about half that: $58,370. Those engaged in research and development earn a median of $96,290, while those working in medical and diagnostic laboratories earn a median annual salary of $79,020. Those employed in hospitals earn a median of $76,670.

Opportunities for Advancement

A scientist who has recently received a PhD is first employed as a postdoctoral researcher, or postdoc. A postdoc is often involved in several projects, overseeing the work of research technicians and students. A postdoc will be first author on any paper resulting from his or her postdoctoral research.

After publishing papers and earning a ranking in the h-index, a postdoc will often be hired as a scientist. Further publications can lead to a promotion to a senior scientist or principal investigator. The next step—normally after several years of experience—is to become a senior group leader. A senior group leader directs a number of scientists working in a specific area of research. Some organizations have a chief scientist who oversees the work of the group leaders and is responsible for the overall output of the laboratory.

What Is the Future Outlook for Medical Research Scientists?

Employment of medical research scientists is projected to grow 8 percent from 2014 to 2024, slightly faster than the average for all occupations (7 percent). A major factor in the future growth of this profession is the aging of the population. A higher number of older people means more cases of chronic diseases such as diabetes, Alzheimer's disease, and cancer. New and more effective treatments for these and other diseases will be greatly needed, keeping medical researchers busy.

Find Out More

American Association for Cancer Research (AACR)
615 Chestnut St., 17th Floor
Philadelphia, PA 19106
website: www.aacr.org

Founded in 1907, the AACR works toward the prevention and cure of cancer by promoting research, education, communication, and collaboration. It publishes several scientific journals as well as *Cancer Today*, a resource for cancer patients, survivors, and caregivers who are seeking information as they or their loved ones face diagnosis, treatment, and life after cancer.

American Society for Clinical Investigation (ASCI)
2015 Manchester Rd.
Ann Arbor, MI 48104
website: www.the-asci.org

Established in 1908, the ASCI is one of the nation's oldest medical research societies. The ASCI seeks to support the scientific efforts, educational needs, and clinical aspirations of physician scientists to improve human health. The ASCI publishes two peer-reviewed journals, *Journal of Clinical Investigation* and *JCI Insight*.

American Society of Gene & Cell Therapy (ASGCT)
website: www.asgct.org

The ASGCT is an organization for scientists, physicians, and other professionals interested in gene and cell therapy. Its mission is to advance knowledge, awareness, and education leading to the discovery and clinical application of gene and cell therapies to alleviate human disease. It publishes the journal *Molecular Therapy*. Its website includes education resources for the general public.

International Society for Stem Cell Research (ISSCR)
5215 Old Orchard Rd., Suite 270
Skokie, IL 60077
website: www.isscr.org

The ISSCR is an association of stem cell scientists and leading authorities on stem cell research and treatments. Its annual meeting attracts more than thirty-five hundred stem cell research professionals each year and provides a forum for scientists to present and discuss their latest research. The ISSCR provides training courses and workshops, and its website includes a jobs board.

Protein Society
PO Box 9397
Glendale, CA 91226
website: www.proteinsociety.org

The Protein Society serves investigators across all disciplines involved in the study of protein structure, function, and design. The society provides forums for scientific collaboration and communication and supports the professional growth of young investigators through workshops and networking opportunities. It publishes the journal *Protein Science*.

Radiation Therapist

Radiation therapists administer ionizing radiation for the treatment of diseases, mainly cancer. To administer the therapy, radiation therapists operate machines called linear accelerators, which direct high-energy X-rays at cancer cells in a patient's body. The radiation can shrink or remove the cancer cells, but it also can damage nearby healthy tissues and organs. To provide safe, accurate, and compassionate treatment to cancer patients, a radiation therapist must possess scientific knowledge, technical expertise, and excellent interpersonal skills. "I went into the field because I loved the technology involved and the relationships you form with your patients," Kaitlyn Ryan, a radiation therapist and the radiation oncology program manager for the nonprofit organization RAD-AID International, told the author of this book. "I love my job."

The complex nature of cancer usually means patients receive treatment from a number of specialists. A radiation therapist is part of a team that includes radiation oncologists (physicians who

At a Glance:

Radiation Therapist

Minimum Educational Requirements
Bachelor's degree or equivalent

Personal Qualities
Problem solving; persistence; good communication skills

Certification and Licensing
Certification required; medical licensing required in twelve states

Working Conditions
Indoors

Salary Range
$55,000 to $121,000

Number of Jobs
As of 2016, about 16,600

Future Job Outlook
Growth rate of 14 percent through 2024

specialize in radiation therapy), medical radiation physicists (physicists who help plan the radiation treatments), medical dosimetrists (specialists responsible for calculating the correct dose of radiation that is used in the treatment), and oncology nurses (registered nurses who specialize in caring for patients with cancer). The radiation therapist is the person who administers the radiation to the patient. Because radiation therapists work directly with patients, they often are the primary link between the patients and other members of the cancer treatment team. "It's a perfect balance between patient care and great technology," Dorothy Hargrove, the chief radiation therapist at Oregon Health & Science University in Portland, Oregon, told *U.S. News & World Report*. Hargrove decided to become a radiation therapist after participating in an internship in radiation therapy. "I watched therapists who knew their patients by name. You got to know patients and be a part of their recovery. It was love at first patient."

Radiation therapy normally extends over a period of several weeks. As a result, radiation therapists must plan the treatment thoroughly and monitor it constantly. As the treatment proceeds, the radiation therapist must recognize changes in the patient's condition and adjust the treatments to increase the odds of a successful treatment.

To provide effective treatment, the radiation therapist must direct high doses of ionizing radiation toward the cancer in the patient's body with a high degree of accuracy. This requires an understanding of human anatomy, human physiology, patient positioning, and treatment techniques. It also requires the ability to operate a computer tomography scanner—a medical imaging technique that creates a three-dimensional image of the target area—before radiation is administered. Karen Lynne Ullman, a radiation therapist at the Center for Cancer Research, National Institutes of Health (NIH) in Bethesda, Maryland, described her typical work day for the NIH Lifeworks website:

> My typical workday involves working with other radiation therapists to treat cancer patients. Radiation therapists are responsible for scheduling patients. We treat patients every 15 minutes. Radiation therapists also operate the Computer Tomography (CT) scanner that is used to plan the patient's radiation therapy.

The CT scanner allows us to view images of the patient's tumor(s) and other internal tissues and organs. The goal of radiation therapy is to kill the cancer cells with as little risk as possible to normal cells. Members of our radiation oncology department work together to treat our patients. This collaborative effort is seen and felt by all, including the patient, family members, and friends.

Once the radiation therapists identify the treatment area and correctly position the patient, they often use immobilization devices so they can place the patient in the same position each time he or she comes in for treatment. They also keep detailed records of the therapy, which usually lasts for several weeks.

Radiation therapists must be skilled in computer technologies, since computers send the correct doses of radiation to the radiation machine. They must know how to check the computer programs to make sure the machine will give the correct dose of radiation to the appropriate area of the patient's body. Because radiation is highly toxic, radiation therapists must possess, use, and maintain knowledge about radiation protection and safety. They examine the radiation machines to make sure they are working properly and follow strict safety procedures to protect themselves and the patients from overexposure to radiation.

How Do You Become a Radiation Therapist?

Education

Radiation therapists can qualify for some positions by completing a one-year certificate program at one of the 120 accredited educational programs recognized by the American Registry of Radiologic Technologists (ARRT). However, many employers prefer to hire candidates who have an associate's degree or a bachelor's degree in radiation therapy. This assures the employer that the radiation therapists have a deep knowledge of human anatomy and physiology, so they can position the patients properly and target the radiation precisely.

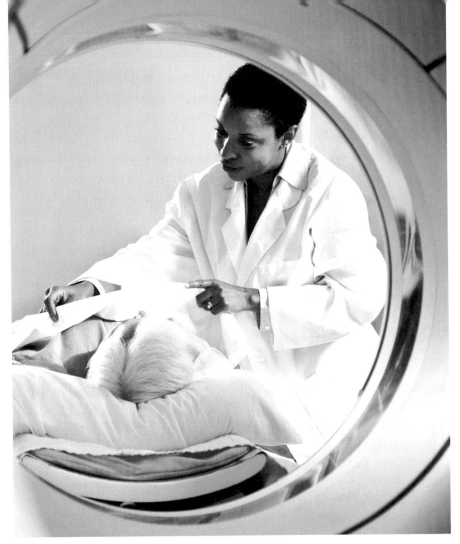

A radiation therapist prepares a cancer patient for a CT scan that will tell the medical team where radiation is needed. Radiation therapists perform these scans and administer ionizing radiation for the treatment of cancer and other diseases.

In addition to courses and clinical experience in how to conduct the procedure, most radiation therapy programs include courses in human anatomy and physiology, physics, algebra, computer science, and research methodology.

Certification and Licensing

More than three-quarters of US states have licensing laws covering the practice of radiologic technology. Requirements vary by state, but thirty-five states use a certification exam administered by the ARRT for licensing purposes. The ARRT exam covers clinical concepts in radiation oncology, treatment planning, treatment delivery, patient care, radiation protection, and quality assurance.

Twelve states—California, Florida, Georgia, Hawaii, Louisiana, Montana, Nevada, New York, North Dakota, Rhode Island, Tennessee, and West Virginia—require health care professionals who have contact with patients to be licensed. Since radiation therapists fall into this category, they must be licensed in those states.

Because radiation therapists spend most of their time giving treatments to individuals who are ill or weakened by cancer, many employers require the therapists to have cardiopulmonary resuscitation or basic life-support certification.

Volunteer Work and Internships

Since radiation therapists must be highly trained, high school students do not have opportunities to volunteer in this profession. However, they can volunteer for job shadowing at a hospital or other health care facility to find out if working with seriously ill patients is something they want to do for a career.

Since clinical experience is required for the completion of many radiation therapy programs, accredited schools usually provide internships for students.

Skills and Personality

Radiation therapists need a wide range of skills to be effective. They need to have an excellent understanding of oncology, radiobiology, radiation physics, radiation oncology techniques, and radiation safety. They also must have good interpersonal and patient-care skills so they are sensitive to the needs of the patient. This includes understanding the psychological and social aspects of cancer. "What I like best about my work is patient contact," says Ullman.

> I often say that it's rare to have a profession where you can hug your patients. I truly think we make the radiation oncology process a lot easier and less complicated for patients and their families. Radiation therapists, as well as the entire department, are vital in making a

very difficult situation much easier. We allay fears by educating the patients and by providing support for him/her and the family. I find that this is the most rewarding aspect of the profession.

Radiation therapists also need good communication skills so they can follow instructions exactly and work effectively with other members of the cancer treatment team, including other health care providers, such as social workers and dietitians.

Radiation therapists need to think critically and use independent judgments as they work. They must be detail oriented, able to follow exact instructions and give the patient the correct amount of radiation. They must enjoy working with highly sophisticated instruments and large machines. Since technology is always changing, they must enjoy continually studying and learning to improve their technical competence and enhance their patient care.

Radiation therapists must have some physical stamina and strength. Typically, they are on their feet for long periods of time. Because some patients may be elderly, disabled, or very weak, the radiation therapist must have the strength to lift and move patients.

On the Job

Employers

According to the Bureau of Labor Statistics (BLS), there were 16,600 radiation therapists employed in 2014. Most work in hospitals, physicians' offices, and outpatient clinics. Some work in medical research laboratories that study cancer treatment, such as the NIH.

Because of the worldwide shortage of radiation therapists, some therapists choose to work abroad. According to the World Health Organization, approximately 4 billion people are at risk for widespread losses and deaths that could be avoided or treated if radiology were available. RAD-AID International, a nonprofit organization based in Chevy Chase, Maryland, offers radiation therapists both paid and unpaid positions overseas. "I was thrilled when I received the fellowship with ASRT/ RAD-AID and was able to travel to China to help out an oncology department in need," Ryan told the author of this book. "A career in radiation therapy can lead to many great things."

Working Conditions

Radiation therapists work indoors in treatment rooms equipped with linear accelerators, computer tomography scanners, and other equipment. Because of the dangers of exposure to radiation and radioactive material, radiation therapists often stand in a different room than the one the patient is in while receiving the radiation.

Most radiation therapists work full time. Since radiation therapy treatments are planned in advance, most radiation therapists work regular hours.

Earnings

According to the BLS, radiation therapists earn good salaries. The median annual wage for radiation therapists was $80,220 in May 2015. The lowest 10 percent earned less than $55,000, and the highest 10 percent earned more than $121,000 per year. The median annual wage for radiation therapists is more than double the median wage for all occupations ($36,200) and about 5 percent higher than the median annual wage of health diagnosing and treating practitioners ($76,760).

Opportunities for Advancement

With additional education, experience, and certification, radiation therapists can become medical dosimetrists. Dosimetrists are specialists who are responsible for calculating the correct dose of radiation used in the treatment of cancer patients.

What Is the Future Outlook for Radiation Therapists?

As the American population ages, the need for radiation therapists will increase, since the risk of cancer is greater for older people. As a result, the BLS estimates the employment of radiation therapists is projected to grow 14 percent from 2014 to 2024, which is more than twice as fast as the average for all occupations for the same period (7 percent). However, since radiation therapy is a small and specialized field, the total number of available positions will grow by only about twenty-three hundred over the ten-year period. The BLS suggests that competition for these high-paying positions will be fierce. "Candidates can expect very strong competition for most radiation therapist positions," states the BLS website. "Jobseekers with prior work experience should have the best job opportunities."

Find Out More

American Registry of Radiologic Technologists (ARRT)
1255 Northland Dr.
St. Paul, MN 55120
website: www.arrt.org

Founded in 1922, the ARRT is the world's largest credentialing organization, certifying and registering professionals in seventeen disciplines. It seeks to ensure high-quality patient care in medical imaging, interventional procedures, and radiation therapy through the administration of education, ethics, and examination requirements.

American Society for Therapeutic Radiology and Oncology (ASTRO)
251 18th St. South, 8th Floor
Arlington, VA 22202
website: www.astro.org

ASTRO is an oncology society with more than ten thousand members who are physicians, nurses, biologists, physicists, radiation therapists, dosimetrists, and other health care professionals who specialize in treating patients with radiation therapies. Its website includes resources for professions to maintain their certification, news, and a special website for radiation patients.

American Society of Radiologic Technologists (ASRT)
15000 Central Ave. SE
Albuquerque, NM 87123
website: www.asrt.org

The ASRT was formed to advance the medical imaging and radiation therapy profession and to enhance the quality and safety of patient care.

Its website offers white papers that examine new or emerging trends in medical imaging or radiation therapy, the results of surveys the organization has taken, radiologic technology news, and information about continuing education.

RAD-AID International
8004 Ellingson Dr.
Chevy Chase, MD 20815
website: www.rad-aid.org

Founded in 2008, RAD-AID International is dedicated to increasing and improving radiology resources in the developing and impoverished countries of the world. The organization networks with organizations worldwide to place radiologic technologists, sonographers, physicians, medical students, residents, and nurses in twenty countries in Africa, Asia, Latin America, and the Caribbean.

Biomedical Engineer

What Does a Biomedical Engineer Do?

Biomedical engineers are behind some of the most exciting medical advances today. These men and women have assisted in the development of artificial limbs controlled by implants in the brain, cochlear implants that improve hearing, and artificial hearts used today. They are currently involved in the creation of artificial eyes, lungs, and livers that will help patients in the near future. Biomedical engineers use cutting-edge technology to aid them in their work; some, for example, use 3-D bioprinters to create artificial ears, cartilage, and blood cells. They also use microscopic technology to fashion nanotubes (measured in billionths of a meter) small enough to slip through a cell's membrane to deliver a payload of drug molecules. All of these medical advances were designed and tested by biomedical engineers.

Biomedical engineers combine engineering principles with biological science to design materials, devices, computer systems, and equipment used in biomedical research and clinical

---

At a Glance:
Biomedical Engineer

Minimum Educational Requirements
Bachelor's degree

Personal Qualities
Ingenuity, creativity, problem solving

Certification and Licensing
Certification required when self-employed; medical licensing required when working with patients

Working Conditions
Indoors

Salary Range
About $51,500 to about $139,500

Number of Jobs
As of 2014, about 22,100

Future Job Outlook
Growth rate of 23 percent through 2024

---

therapy. They often bring together knowledge from several areas to solve clinical problems. Hicham Fenniri, a bioengineering professor at Northeastern University in Boston who works in nanomedicine, told the author of this book how his work combines his interest in DNA, nanotechnology, and engineering:

> Since its discovery in the early 1950s, the DNA double helix has inspired countless scientific and engineering developments, from the sequencing of the human genome to the discovery of the genetic basis of cancer. Many researchers working at the interface of science and engineering, like myself, were inspired by the architecture of the double helix and the simplicity of its design. These features inspired much of the work that I have done in the past 20 years. My research group has developed new synthetic molecules that self-assemble spontaneously (just like DNA) into well-defined nanotubular architectures. This approach allows us to exquisitely control the chemical, physical, and biological properties of the resulting architectures, as well as their dimensions, for possible use in drug delivery into targeted cells.

Bioengineers usually specialize in a single, narrow field. For example, bioinstrumentation engineers use electronics and computer science to create ultrasensitive sensors and measurement devices used to diagnose and treat diseases. Biomaterial engineers study how human-made and naturally occurring materials interact with living organisms, applying this knowledge to design and test implantable devices and materials. Biomechanics engineers apply the principles of mechanics to understand and solve biological and medical problems. Clinical engineers support patient care by applying engineering and managerial skills to health care technology. In a hospital setting, a clinical engineer often functions as the technology manager for medical equipment systems. Orthopedic engineers design artificial joints, devise improvements to prosthetics, and aid in the development of biomaterials that can be used to replace damaged or diseased bones, cartilage, intervertebral discs, tendons, and ligaments. Rehabilitation engineers use engineering science to develop technological solutions and devices to assist individuals with disabilities and to aid the recovery of physical and cognitive functions lost because of disease or injury.

The day-to-day duties of a biological engineer depend on the field in which he or she works. For example, biomaterial engineers working in the research and development laboratory of a medical device company might work on designs and improvements for implantable equipment and devices, such as artificial internal organs. A clinical engineer working in a hospital might install, adjust, maintain, repair, or provide technical support for biomedical equipment. An engineer working in a research laboratory might perform experiments, write technical reports, publish research papers, and make recommendations based on their research findings, while an engineer working in the pharmaceutical industry might create computer models of drug therapies or work on new drug delivery systems.

How Do You Become a Biomedical Engineer?

Education

Just as the responsibilities of a biomedical engineer vary widely, so, too, do the educational requirements needed for the different jobs. Any entry-level engineer working on mechanical devices, electronics, or software programs might need only a bachelor's degree in biomedical engineering or bioengineering from a program accredited by the Accreditation Board for Engineering and Technology in order to enter the occupation. Accredited biomedical engineering programs are interdisciplinary, meaning they combine different disciplines or areas of study, including biology, engineering, and computing. Coursework typically includes life sciences courses, such as anatomy and physiology; engineering courses, such as fluid and solid mechanics; and computing courses, such as programming and circuit design. Accredited programs also include substantial training in engineering design. In addition to classroom study, a biomedical engineering program often involves laboratory work so students gain experience in the practical application of their knowledge.

Many of the advanced fields of biomedical engineering require graduate degrees, especially PhDs. To engineer genes, stem cells, nanotechnology, and other complex biological and physical materials, the biomedical engineer needs a deep understanding of the science behind the technology and the biological problems he or she is trying to solve. This level of knowledge and understanding typically comes only with graduate studies. Students interested in a career in biomedical engineering might have a bachelor's degree in engineering, computer science, or the life sciences, and then specialize in biomedical engineering in graduate school.

High school students interested in biomedical engineering should mimic the college curriculum and take a range of science courses, such as biology, chemistry, physics, and computer science. They should also take math courses, including algebra, geometry, trigonometry, statistics, and calculus. Courses in practical applications such as drafting, mechanical drawing, and computer graphics would contribute to a strong foundation for a college career in biomedical engineering.

Certification and Licensing

Biomedical engineers who are privately employed normally do not need to be licensed, unless they work directly with medical patients. However, biomedical engineers who work as consultants or offer their services to the public need to be licensed. Engineers are licensed at the state level by professional licensing boards. Engineering boards confer the professional engineer license when licensure candidates meet a combination of requirements in education, experience, and exams.

Licensing requirements vary by state, but the process usually includes passing two exams administered by the National Council of Examiners for Engineering and Surveying. The first exam is the Fundamentals of Engineering exam, which can be taken by a student who is nearing graduation in biomedical engineering. The second exam is the Principles and Practice of Engineering (PE) exam. To qualify for the PE exam, a biomedical engineer must have at least four years of work experience. PE exams are offered in different specialties, but there is no PE exam specifically for biomedical engineers. Biomedical engineers must choose another specialty, such as agricultural and biological, chemical, computer, electrical and electronics, mechanical systems and materials, or thermal and fluids systems. Those who achieve a passing score on the PE exam are licensed as a professional engineer.

Volunteer Work and Internships

The Biomedical Engineering Society (BMES) offers biomedical students the opportunity to volunteer within the field they are studying. According to the BMES, volunteering helps students to gain experience, network, and discover new ideas. The BMES also offers internships, which allow students to gain work experience, expand their knowledge, and build their skills. Many private companies, colleges, universities, and government-run labs offer internships as well.

Skills and Personal Qualities

Biomedical engineers must have excellent analytical skills to pinpoint medical or biological problems and design appropriate solutions. They also must be creative thinkers to combine information in new ways to create innovative equipment, devices, and therapies to treat diseases or medical conditions. Typically, biomedical engineers employ advanced mathematics such as calculus and statistics to analyze complex biological systems and design medical technologies. Biomedical engineers usually work in teams with scientists, health care workers, or other engineers, so they need good communication skills.

On the Job

Employers

According to the Bureau of Labor Statistics (BLS), biomedical engineers held about twenty-two thousand jobs in 2014. The majority were employed in five industries: medical equipment and supplies manufacturing (23 percent); research and development (16 percent); pharmaceutical manufacturing (12 percent); measuring, electromedical, and instruments manufacturing (8 percent); and hospitals (8 percent).

Working Conditions

Biomedical engineers work indoors in a wide range of settings, including universities, hospitals, research and development facilities of companies, and government regulatory agencies. They spend the majority of their time in their offices, analyzing problems and designing solutions by hand or on a computer. They may spend time in a laboratory or in a fabricating facility where parts are made and designs take physical form.

Biomedical engineers usually work full time on a normal schedule. However, biomedical engineers sometimes may have to work evenings and weekends to meet deadlines or to monitor experiments or the testing of prototypes.

Earnings

Biomedical engineers earn incomes far above the national average of all occupations. According to the BLS, the median annual wage for biomedical engineers was $86,220 in May 2015. That is 2.38 times as much as the median annual wage for all occupations. The lowest 10 percent of biomedical engineers earned less than $51,500 per year, while the highest 10 percent earned more than $139,000.

Median incomes of biomedical engineers vary greatly depending on the industry in which they are employed. In May 2015 those working in research and development in the physical, engineering, and life sciences sectors earned a median annual wage 33 percent greater than those working in hospitals—$97,100 compared to $72,950. Of course, it is not just the location, but also the nature of the work that dictates the salary. Those working on the frontiers of biomedical technology earn more than those who purchase, install, organize, and maintain machinery and devices that already exist. Biomedical engineers working in the medical equipment and supplies manufacturing sector earned a median annual wage of $91,030 in 2015, while those in the pharmaceutical and medicine manufacturing industries earned a median annual wage of $81,750.

Opportunities for Advancement

Advancement in biomedical engineering is as varied as the work settings. Those in college and university laboratories may follow the academic career path: assistant professor, associate professor, full professor, department chair. Those in research laboratories might follow the scientific path: scientist, senior scientist, principal investigator, group leader, chief scientist. Those in corporate settings might progress from engineer to senior engineer, and then to principal engineer. Biomedical engineers who earn a master's degree in business administration might move into corporate management positions, overseeing the development of a product line or taking part in strategic planning.

What Is the Future Outlook for Biomedical Engineers?

According to the BLS, employment of biomedical engineers is projected to grow 23 percent from 2014 to 2024, more than three times faster than the average for all occupations. Biomedical engineers will be in high demand because of the growing need for artificial organs, limbs, and joints by the growing number of older Americans. In addition, the large number of older people will require prosthetics, medical devices, and advanced therapies such as gene therapy and stem cell therapy to combat diseases that are more prevalent in older populations, such as cancer, Alzheimer's disease, and heart disease.

Find Out More

Accreditation Board for Engineering and Technology (ABET)
415 North Charles St.
Baltimore, MD 21201
website: www.abet.org

A nonprofit, nongovernmental organization recognized by the Council for Higher Education Accreditation, ABET accredits college and university programs in the disciplines of applied science, computing, engineering, and engineering technology at the associate's, bachelor's, and master's degree levels.

American Institute for Medical and Biological Engineering (AIMBE)
1400 I St. NW, Suite 235
Washington, DC 20005
website: http://navigate.aimbe.org

The AIMBE is a nonprofit organization that advocates for fifty thousand individuals and the top 2 percent of medical and biological engineers. Its "Navigate the Circuit" website is designed to help students of all levels on their path to medical and biological engineering with sections on "Why Bioengineering?," "Meet Inspiring Bioengineers," "Career Pathways," and "Tools for Success."

Biomedical Engineering Society (BMES)
8201 Corporate Dr., Suite 1125
Landover, MD 20785
website: www.bmes.org

The BMES is the world's leading society of professionals devoted to developing and using engineering and technology to advance human health. It communicates recent advances, discoveries, and inventions through journals and conferences and promotes education and professional development through workshops and e-learning.

National Institute of Biomedical Imaging and Bioengineering (NIBIB)
9000 Rockville Pike
Bethesda, MD 20892
website: www. nibib.nih.gov

Part of the National Institutes of Health, the NIBIB seeks to improve health through research and development of new biomedical imaging and bioengineering techniques and devices to fundamentally improve the detection, treatment, and prevention of disease. The website includes resource links for students, parents, and teachers; news and videos; and training information.

Robot-Assisted Surgeon

What Does a Robot-Assisted Surgeon Do?

Robot-assisted surgeons are physicians who perform operations using high-tech robotic equipment. The robotic equipment allows the surgeon to perform many procedures with greater precision, flexibility, and control than is possible with conventional techniques. Robotic surgery is usually associated with minimally invasive surgery—procedures performed through tiny incisions—although it can also be used in traditional open surgical procedures, such as heart surgery. Robot-assisted surgery often results in fewer complications, less pain and blood loss, quicker recovery, and smaller, less noticeable scars than is possible with traditional surgery.

In the most common type of robot-assisted surgery, known as remote surgery or telesurgery, the surgeon sits at a computer console near the operating table. One mechanical arm equipped with a camera and

---

At a Glance:
Robot-Assisted Surgeon

Minimum Educational Requirements
MD

Personal Qualities
Physical dexterity; excellent interpersonal and communication skills

Certification and Licensing
Medical license required

Working Conditions
Indoors

Salary Range
About $395,000*

Number of Jobs
46,000*

Future Job Outlook
20 percent through 2024*

*Numbers are for all surgeons, a group that includes robot-assisted surgeons.

other mechanical arms with surgical instruments attached to them are located by the operating table. The imaging equipment gives the surgeon a high-definition, magnified, 3-D view of the surgical site. Outfitted with a telemanipulator, which transmits the surgeon's motions to robotic arms, the surgeon moves his or her hands to guide the robotic arms and perform the procedure.

The robotic arms can access the body more easily through small incisions than a surgeon can. The equipment also integrates large amounts of data and images, allowing the surgeon to access areas deep within the body with precision. The robotic equipment filters out hand tremors and scales the surgeon's large movements into smaller ones inside the patient, allowing robot-assisted surgeons to perform complex procedures with more precision, flexibility, and control than is possible by hand. David B. Samadi, chief of robotic surgery at Lenox Hill Hospital in New York City and a practicing urologist who has performed more than seven thousand robot-assisted prostate surgeries, discussed the advantages of robotic surgery in a presentation to urologists at Times Center in New York that was recorded and posted on YouTube:

> I think of robotic surgery as an extension of my arms. We're working in a very narrow space with a prostate that is surrounded by sensitive nerves attached to the many organs. The robot allows me to be able to move in a finite area, being able to work in a bloodless field. If there is no blood in the field, I can really see what we're doing. With the magnification of the camera, you can save the nerves.

Another, even more advanced form of robotic surgery is known as supervisory-controlled surgery. With this system, the operation is preformed solely by the robot, which proceeds according to computerized instructions created by the surgeon before the procedure. In supervisory-controlled surgery, the surgeon plans the procedure and oversees the operation, but does not partake in it directly. Because the robot performs the entire procedure, each operation must be individually programmed for the surgery using 3-D images and data from the patient.

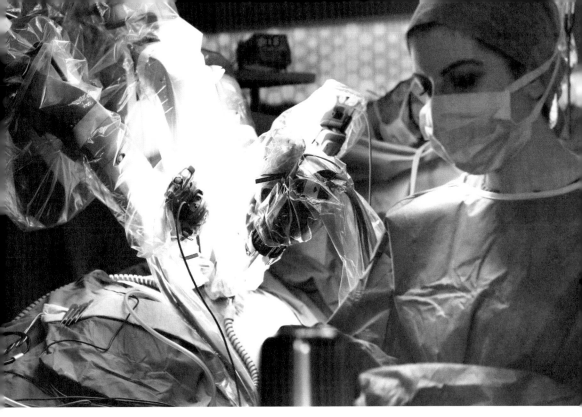

Using high-tech robotic equipment, a surgeon performs a minimally invasive operation on a patient. Robotic equipment gives surgeons more flexibility and control and often results in fewer complications, less pain and blood loss, and quicker recovery for patients.

Like traditional surgeons, robot-assisted surgeons treat injuries, diseases, and deformities using a variety of instruments to remove or reshape tissue or implant a device. While many traditional surgeons perform general surgery, most robot-assisted surgeons specialize in a narrow area, such as cardiothoracic surgery (treatment of the heart or lungs), gynecological surgery (treatment of the female reproductive system), neurological surgery (treatment of the brain and nervous system), ophthalmic surgery (treatment of the eyes), orthopedic surgery (the treatment of the musculoskeletal system), and urological surgery (treatment of the urinary system and the male reproductive system).

Robotic surgery involves risks similar to those of conventional open surgery, such as the risk of infection. However, it may be possible in the future to lower the risk of infection by placing the patient in a clean room, which has a controlled level of particles and pathogens in the air, while the robot-assisted surgeon operates from another location. Robot-assisted surgery presents unique risks, however. Because robotic surgeries involve many integrated pieces of equipment, including sensors, imaging equipment, the robotic arms, and the computerized equipment at the surgeon's console, an equipment malfunction can be dangerous or even fatal. The makers of equipment have tried to address these risks by including redundant sensors and robot movement barriers to prevent the robotic arms from moving beyond a confined site, but these safety features increase cost, making them inaccessible to some physicians.

How Do You Become a Robot-Assisted Surgeon?

Education

Surgeons, like all physicians, must meet rigorous education and training requirements. Almost all physicians complete at least four years of undergraduate school, four years of medical school, and three to seven years in internship and residency programs, depending on their specialty. Surgeons generally require more years in residency than other specialties. Some medical schools offer combined undergraduate and medical school programs that typically last six or seven years.

Admission to medical schools is competitive. First, the applicant must have at least a bachelor's degree, although many candidates also have advanced degrees. Next, applicants must submit transcripts, scores from the Medical College Admission Test, and letters of recommendation. Most medical schools require applicants to interview with members of the admissions committee. Committee members often assess an applicant's personal qualities, including leadership and interpersonal skills.

Undergraduate premed students normally take courses in biology, anatomy, chemistry, physics, and math. Once they enter medical school, medical students spend much of the first two years taking courses such as anatomy, biochemistry, pharmacology, psychology, medical ethics, and the laws governing medicine. In their last two years of medical school, students normally spend their time in "clinicals"—training sessions in hospitals and clinics where they work with patients under the supervision of experienced physicians. Medical students are required to work in different areas of medical practice, such as emergency room, family practice, internal medicine, obstetrics and gynecology, pediatrics, psychiatry, and surgery, so they gain experience in diagnosing and treating illnesses in a variety of environments and can choose the specialty that appeals to them.

Certification and Licensing

All states require physicians and surgeons to be licensed. To qualify for a license, physicians must graduate from an accredited medical school and complete residency training in their specialty. They also must pass the United States Medical Licensing Examination before being permitted to practice medicine in the United States.

Certification is not required for surgeons, but it often increases their employment opportunities. To become board certified, a surgeon must complete a residency program and pass a specialty certification exam from the American Board of Medical Specialties or the American Board of Physician Specialties.

Volunteer Work and Internships

High school students interested in robotic surgery should apply for internships at hospitals to gain exposure to the medical environment and to find out if the medical profession is suitable for them. In addition, participating in science fairs is a good way to learn about robotics and robot controls. Undergraduate students in premed programs are offered many opportunities for volunteer programs, including internships at hospitals.

Skills and Personal Qualities

Robot-assisted surgeons need to have many skills and qualities. They must have a high degree of physical dexterity, since in most cases they guide the robot's movements by moving their own hands. All surgery—especially microsurgery—requires the surgeon to have very fine motor skills. Robot-assisted surgeons also must be comfortable adapting to change and working with the new technology.

John F. Dulemba, a gynecological surgeon in Denton, Texas, told the author of this book:

> I flew helicopters in the army, including in Vietnam, and started medical school at age thirty. In my medical training, I saw wonderfully skilled doctors, but most of them had been doing the same thing for twenty years. I never wanted to be stagnant in my career. I vowed to myself to try and move forward and learn new things. When the robot came along, I was as resistant as many others, but I tried it. Once I sat down at the console, I found the movements are similar to those of flying a helicopter or operating a flight simulator, and I immediately saw the benefits over standard surgery. I love robotic surgery. If ever a person and a machine were made for each other, the surgical robot and I were.

Like all physicians, surgeons must have excellent interpersonal skills. They must be able to listen carefully to patients to fully understand their symptoms. They must be able to communicate clearly with patients as well as with other members of the health care staff. They also need to have compassion for patients, who are sick or injured and often are in pain. Surgeons also must have patience and empathy for patients who are fearful or apprehensive about undergoing surgery.

Robot-assisted surgeons need excellent problem-solving skills to evaluate patients' conditions and determine the appropriate treatments. If problems occur during the surgery, the surgeon must be able to analyze the cause and remedy the situation quickly. Surgeons are the leaders of their surgical teams, so they must have leadership skills both in the operating room and as they manage the practices.

On the Job

Employers

According to the Bureau of Labor Statistics (BLS), surgeons held about forty-six thousand jobs in 2014, with robot-assisted surgeons making up a fraction of the total number. Many robot-assisted surgeons work in private offices or clinics, often with a small staff of nurses and administrative personnel. However, they usually are affiliated with hospitals with operating rooms equipped with robotic surgery equipment.

Most robot-assisted surgeons work full time. Because the surgeries must be planned in advance, such surgeons normally work regular hours. However, if a patient develops complications after the operation, the surgeon may need to make an emergency visit to the hospital.

Earnings

Surgeons are among the highest-paid professionals in the United States. According to the Medical Group Management Association's Physician Compensation and Production Survey, the median annual wage for all surgeons was $395,456 in 2014—more than ten times the median wage for all occupations.

Opportunities for Advancement

Robot-assisted surgeons typically are at the top of their profession. The only possibility for advancement is to become the chief surgeon of a hospital or clinic. The chief surgeon oversees the daily activities within the surgical unit. He or she is responsible for hiring surgeons and for supervising and motivating all members of the staff.

Some robot-assisted surgeons serve as consultants to equipment manufacturers, testing and fine-tuning robotic surgery equipment.

What Is the Future Outlook for Robot-Assisted Surgeons?

According to the BLS, employment of surgeons is projected to grow 20 percent from 2014 to 2024, about three times faster than the average for all occupations (7 percent). The aging US population is expected to increase the demand for surgical services, since older people have high rates of chronic diseases such as prostate, uterine, and bladder cancer, all of which are easier to access and remove using robot-assisted surgical techniques.

Some experts believe technological advances will allow surgeons to see more patients in the same amount of time, reducing the number of surgeons who would be needed to perform the same tasks. Others argue that the increasing number of individuals accessing health insurance because of federal health insurance reform will increase demand for the services of surgeons.

Find Out More

All About Robotic Surgery
website: http://allaboutroboticsurgery.com

Sponsored by AVRA Medical Robotics Inc., the website offers news about robotic surgery, links to training courses, profiles of robot-assisted surgeons, and videos of various robot-assisted procedures. The "Medical Robotics Books & Scholarly Articles" includes abstracts of articles about robotic surgery and summaries of books on the topic.

American College of Surgeons (ACS)
633 N. Saint Clair St.
Chicago, IL 60611
website: www.facs.org

Founded in 1913, the ACS is a scientific and educational association of surgeons dedicated to improving the quality of care for the surgical patient by setting high standards for surgical education and practice. The college sponsors a variety of continuing medical education programs to help surgeons keep up to date on the latest information on surgical subjects.

Clinical Robotic Surgery Association (CRSA)
2 Prudential Plaza
180 N. Stetson, Suite 3500
Chicago, IL 60601
website: www.clinicalrobotics.com

The CRSA provides clinical, educational, and innovative services to robot-assisted surgeons. Its website features a video portal that shows hundreds of actual surgical procedures as well as discussions and presentations that have been posted by members. The association also sponsors events that give surgeons the opportunity to learn about advances in robotic surgery.

Biological Technician

What Does a Biological Technician Do?

Biological technicians, also known as research technicians or research associates, perform much of the hands-on work in biomedical research laboratories. They set up, maintain, test, and clean laboratory tools—from traditional instruments such as microscopes, test tubes, and petri dishes to advanced equipment, such as gene sequencing machines that can perform thousands or even millions of operations per hour in a process known as high-throughput sequencing. Biological technicians also obtain and prepare biological samples and reagents for experiments, conduct tests, and document the results. Some of these experiments may involve cultures of living microbes, which are grown in petri dishes and stained to aid in their identification when viewed through a microscope. In some cases, the biological technician may interpret the data and offer a preliminary analysis of the results. "I am a drug discoverer, so my job is to help find the next generation of antibiotics," Nikki Carter, a research associate with Cubist Pharmaceuticals, told the Science Buddies website.

At a Glance:

Biological Technician

Minimum Educational Requirements
Bachelor's degree

Personal Qualities
Strong analytical skills; detail oriented

Certification and Licensing
Licensing required in twelve states when working with patients or patient samples

Working Conditions
Indoors

Salary Range
About $27,000 to $69,000

Number of Jobs
As of 2014, about 79,000

Future Job Outlook
Growth rate of 5 percent through 2024

41

Most of my day is spent in the lab running Minimal Inhibitory Concentration assays or MICs for short. Chemists make compounds that could be the next new antibiotic and pass them along to me for testing against some really serious and potentially dangerous bacteria. To test these compounds, I make serial dilutions and add different bacterial strains to them. The bacteria grow overnight, and I look at the results the next morning. The best compounds are those that kill the bacteria using the smallest amount of compound possible—this is what it means to be potent. Some of the bacteria we are trying to make antibiotics for are ones that are found in hospitals that are resistant to current antibiotics; these are sometimes called Superbugs. Finding new ways to treat resistant bacteria, or Superbugs, is really important.

Biological technicians are part of an investigative team searching for clues to the causes of human diseases and developing new therapies to prevent and treat them. The team is led by a biomedical scientist, who directs the research and designs the experiments. The biological technician receives written and oral instructions for the experimentation, procures the items needed, prepares the equipment, and runs the tests. Says Remy Thomas, a research technician at Qatar Biomedical Research Institute, Hamad bin Khalifa University in Doha, Qatar:

As part of a research team, a research technician has an exciting opportunity to write standard operating procedures for the experiments, establish protocols [sets of instructions that allow scientists to recreate experiments in their own laboratory], maintain inventory of items used in the experiments, keep detailed records, and to present the data in scientific meetings and conferences. There is often troubleshooting that needs to be done on experiments. You are expected to have the patience and persistence, especially when your experiments don't work. But the most exciting

At work in a biomedical research lab, a biological technician performs a variety of tasks. These include setting up, maintaining, testing, and cleaning laboratory tools; preparing biological samples for experiments; conducting tests; and documenting results.

part is when your project is going in the right direction and you get the feeling that you have positively contributed to the society.

Biological technicians often operate highly sophisticated laboratory equipment, such as electron microscopes, single-cell microfluidics platforms, and flow cytometers, which segregate specific cells (such as cancer cells) for high-throughput analysis. Many of these devices produce digital output, so the biological technician must use computer software to collect and analyze the experimental data. Peggy Hall, a biological technician at the Intramural Sequencing Center, National Human Genome Research Institute, National Institutes of Health, described her typical day to the NIH Lifeworks website:

> My typical workday involves constructing a deoxyribonucleic acid (or DNA) library. It is a way of taking a long string of DNA and breaking it up into small pieces (a library), which we can study further. This is just one step in a series of steps to do large scale DNA sequencing. In our section of the National Intramural Sequencing Center (NISC), we receive DNA samples in a glycerol stock from different sources. My favorite work was the computer analysis I did when I was in the finishing section. We have a software program to analyze the DNA sequences. I reviewed the sequence data to make sure it was complete. If the sequence was not good, I suggested methods to use to improve that sequence area.

How Do You Become a Biological Technician?

Education

Biological technicians need to have at least a bachelor's degree in one of the biological sciences. Some of the more prestigious laboratories require a master's degree in biology or a closely related field. Biological technicians with a background in fields such as microbiology, chemistry, mathematics, biotechnology, cell biology, neuroscience, molecular biology, biochemistry, or physics will have more employment options. A biological technician who wants to work in genomics, proteomics, and metabolomics and other fields that use computers to model biological processes should take computer science courses. Successful candidates usually take courses that include laboratory coursework, with an emphasis on bench skills. "If students have an opportunity during the bachelor's or master's program to work on a specific project in a research lab, they should take it so they can learn what it is like to work in a lab," says Dr. Thomas. "It is a good chance for them to assess if they would like to pursue a career in research."

Certification and Licensing

Biological technicians who work in laboratories operated and maintained exclusively for research do not have to be licensed, unless they conduct research with human patients or live animals. Technicians whose work involves patients or public health must be licensed in thirteen states and territories: California, Florida, Georgia, Hawaii, Louisiana, Montana, Nevada, New York, North Dakota, Puerto Rico, Rhode Island, Tennessee, and West Virginia. Licensing is available through state boards of occupational licensure or departments of health. Licensing requirements vary by state and the technician's specialty.

Although certification is not required to enter the occupation in all cases, many employers prefer to hire certified technicians. Many colleges offer certificate programs in biotechnology. These programs can be taken while the student is pursuing a bachelor's degree or after graduation. Certification programs offer students a chance to gain more laboratory experience than they would in an undergraduate program without enrolling in graduate school to obtain a master's degree. Certification indicates to prospective employers that the candidate has mastered the research techniques needed in a career as a biological technician.

Volunteer Work and Internships

Many medical schools and research laboratories offer internships for undergraduate students interested in biological technology. For example, Rockefeller University offers a Summer Undergraduate Research Fellowship program that enables undergraduates to work with scientists and conduct laboratory research in a broad range of areas, including biochemistry, structural biology and chemistry, molecular biology, immunology, virology, microbiology, neuroscience, and mathematical biology. Experience performing hands-on work in a research laboratory can be a tremendous advantage when applying for a permanent position after graduation.

Skills and Personal Qualities

Biological technicians need to be detail oriented in order to conduct scientific experiments with precision and keep complete, accurate records of their work. They must have excellent communication skills so they can follow the instructions of lead scientists and then communicate their findings in written reports, noting the conditions under which the experiment was carried out, the procedures they followed, and the results they obtained. "Good communication between the team members is very important to discuss protocols, update inventory lists, and keep the research moving forward," says Dr. Thomas.

Biological technicians need good technical skills to properly operate and maintain sophisticated equipment. "One of the most important skills that the biological technician should possess is the ability to operate different instruments in the lab," says Dr. Thomas. "There are a lot of high-throughput instruments in a research lab which need a great deal of maintenance, including calibration, on a regular basis. As the operator of the instrument, you should also be well trained in the maintenance and the troubleshooting of these instruments."

On the Job

Employers

There were about seventy-nine thousand biological technicians employed in 2014. The majority worked in four major industries: About 26 percent worked in public and private colleges, universities, and professional schools; another 26 percent worked in research and development in physical, engineering, and life sciences; about 12 percent worked in agencies of the federal government, such as the Department of Health and Human Services and the Department of Agriculture; about 9 percent worked in chemical manufacturing.

Working Conditions

Biological technicians who work in the medical field typically work indoors in laboratories and offices, where they conduct experiments and analyze the results under the supervision of medical scientists and research assistants. Since they often handle biological samples, dangerous organisms, and other hazardous materials, biological technicians must follow strict procedures and wear special clothing, known as a clean-room suit, to avoid contaminating themselves or the environment. In some cases, they may work in a laboratory known as a cleanroom, which has a controlled number of airborne pollutants such as dust, microbes, aerosol particles, and chemical vapors. "When I am in the lab, I do most of my work in a biological safety cabinet (BSC)," says Carter. "The BSC helps keep everything I am working on sterile and keeps me safe from the bacteria. Safety is a top priority, so in the lab it is important that I wear my lab coat, safety glasses, and gloves."

Earnings

The median annual wage for biological technicians was $41,650 in May 2015. This salary is about 15 percent higher than the median wage for all occupations. The lowest 10 percent of biological technicians earned less than $26,610 per year, while the highest 10 percent earned more than $69,000. Chemical manufacturing is the top-paying industry for biological technicians with a median annual salary of $47,760. Research and development positions paid a median of $45,220. Biological technicians employed by private colleges, universities, and professional schools earned a median annual salary of $45,220, while those at state schools earned slightly less: $39,030. Those employed by the federal government earned a median annual salary of $35,610.

Opportunities for Advancement

Biological technicians can be hired at the entry level. Biological technicians who are licensed to handle patient samples and work in the health care sector are sometimes referred to as medical technologists. With additional experience and education, a biological technician can become a research associate, taking on more of the experimental responsibilities in a research laboratory. Graduates with a bachelor's degree often qualify for these positions, but most require master's, doctoral, or postdoctoral education.

What Is the Future Outlook for Biological Technicians?

Employment of biological technicians is projected to grow 5 percent from 2014 to 2024, which is not quite as fast as the average for all occupations. The expected growth in biotechnology and medical research will fuel the demand for qualified biological technicians, since they help scientists develop new treatments for diseases, such as diabetes, cancer, and Alzheimer's disease. Graduates entering the field should expect strong competition because of the large number of bachelor's degrees being awarded in biology and related fields. Those with strong laboratory experience, especially gained through internships in respected research laboratories, will find the best opportunities.

Find Out More

American Association for Clinical Chemistry (AACC)
900 Seventh St. NW, Suite 400
Washington, DC 20001
website: www.aacc.org

The AACC is a global scientific and medical professional organization dedicated to clinical laboratory science and its application to health care. The organization publishes journals—*Clinical Chemistry* and the *Journal of Applied Laboratory Medicine*—and two newsletters. It offers its members certification programs, continuing education courses, and job listings.

Association for Molecular Pathology (AMP)
9650 Rockville Pike, Suite E133
Bethesda, MD 20814
website: www.amp.org

The AMP was founded in 1995 to provide structure and leadership to the emerging field of molecular diagnostics. Its twenty-three hundred members include pathologists and doctoral scientist laboratory directors; basic and translational scientists; technologists; and trainees. It offers live training, online courses, and webinars. It lists accredited organizations for certification in molecular pathology.

Association for the Advancement of Medical Instrumentation (AAMI)
4301 N. Fairfax Dr., Suite 301
Arlington, VA 22203
website: www.aami.org

Founded in 1967, the AAMI is a nonprofit organization dedicated to the development, management, and use of safe and effective health care technology. The organization provides its members with courses, conferences, and continuing education, including certification programs. It publishes weekly and monthly newsletters and a bimonthly peer-reviewed journal.

Association of Biomolecular Resource Facilities (ABRF)
9650 Rockville Pike
Bethesda, MD 20814
website: www.abrf.org

The ABRF is an international society dedicated to advancing core and research biotechnology laboratories through research, communication, and education. The ABRF offers conferences, a quarterly journal, and publication of research group studies. The society also sponsors research studies designed to help members incorporate new biotechnologies into their laboratories.

Diagnostic Medical Sonographer

What Does a Diagnostic Medical Sonographer Do?

At a Glance:
Diagnostic Medical Sonographer

Minimum Educational Requirements
Associate's degree or equivalent

Personal Qualities
Detail oriented; good hand-eye coordination; strong interpersonal skills

Certification and Licensing
Certification required; licensing required in some states

Working Conditions
Indoors

Salary Range
About $49,000 to $97,000

Number of Jobs
As of 2014, about 60,700

Future Job Outlook
Growth rate of about 26 percent through 2024

Diagnostic sonographers, also known as ultrasound technologists, use equipment that emits high-frequency sound waves that penetrate the body to create an image of the tissue beneath the skin. These images are known as sonograms, or ultrasounds. Physicians use sonograms to "see" inside the body and diagnose problems. Because the process is painless and the results are available in real time, sonography is often the first imaging test performed when disease is suspected or an injury has occurred beneath the skin. "I love being a diagnostic medical sonographer," Marta Thorup, a diagnostic medical sonographer at Dosher Memorial Hospital in Southport, North Carolina, told the author of this book. "It provides me the opportunity to work as a part of a team in solving diagnostic dilemmas and answering medical questions that have a significant impact on patient outcome. I feel like I have the best career in the hospital."

To conduct a test, a sonographer places an instrument called an ultrasound transducer, or probe, onto the skin of a patient and directs the sound waves into the body. Because the sound waves are at a frequency higher than human hearing, the sounds are not heard by the sonographer or the patient. Some of the sound waves passing through the body are reflected back to the probe, which relays the "echo" information to the machine that creates the image. The machine measures the time it takes to receive the echo, and then plots the location of the tissue on a screen. In a typical ultrasound, millions of pulses are sent and received each second. Since dense tissue reflects more sound waves, it creates a brighter image on the screen. Less dense tissue reflects fewer sound waves and creates dim or dark areas on the screen. The combination of light and dark areas creates a two-dimensional image of the targeted area inside the body.

While watching the screen, the sonographer moves the probe along the surface of the body at different angles to obtain various views. Sonographers are trained to recognize the difference between normal and abnormal tissue so they can direct the probe to capture the information the physician will need for the diagnosis.

Diagnostic medical sonographers perform many duties in addition to conducting the ultrasound test. They take a patient's medical history, answer any questions the patient has about the procedure, and prepare the surface of the body to be analyzed by coating the area with a gel that helps conduct the sound waves through the skin. Sonographers also set up the imaging equipment and make sure it is working properly. After the test, the sonographer reviews the images to ensure they will provide adequate views of the areas being tested. The sonographer records the findings, enters them into the patient's records, and provides the physician with a summary of the diagnostic information.

Many sonographers specialize in one area of the body or type of patient. Abdominal sonographers specialize in imaging a patient's abdominal cavity and organs, such as the liver, gallbladder, pancreas, spleen, aorta, or kidneys. Breast sonographers carefully evaluate breast tissue for the cause of palpable lumps or the cause of a dense finding on a mammogram. They look for benign and malignant tumors in the breast tissue and help physicians track the growth of tumors.

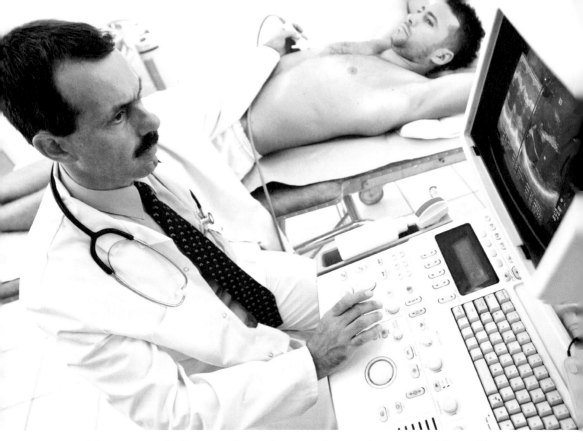

A diagnostic medical sonographer performs an ultrasound on a patient's heart. The image, or sonogram, allows doctors to "see" inside the body and diagnose problems.

Cardiovascular sonographers create images of the heart, checking the function of the heart muscle, valves, and chambers; they often assist with surgical procedures. Intervention sonographers help guide the needle for the interventional radiologist or surgeon to perform biopsies or draining fluids from the body. Musculoskeletal sonographers examine muscles, ligaments, tendons, and joints. They can assist the physician in determining what is causing motion-induced symptoms and often help guide physicians so they can deliver injections to the best areas for treatment. Obstetric and gynecologic sonographers specialize in imaging the female reproductive system, including the uterus and ovaries. In a pregnant female, sonographers track the baby's growth and health. Pediatric sonographers specialize in imaging infants and children, often in cases that involve premature birth or birth defects. Small-part sonographers create diagnostic images of the thyroid gland and testicles looking for benign or malignant diseases. Vascular sonographers create images of the veins and arteries, collecting data that can help physicians diagnose disorders affecting blood flow.

How Do You Become a Diagnostic Medical Sonographer?

Education

Students who want to pursue this career need to find an education program accredited by the Commission on Accreditation of Allied Health Education Programs so they can qualify to take the American Registry for Diagnostic Medical Sonography (ARDMS) certification exam, which is required by most employers. Most students attend an accredited college or university to obtain a two-year associate's degree or a four-year bachelor's degree in the field. College programs usually include courses in anatomy, medical terminology, and related life sciences. Most undergraduate programs also offer clinical experience, allowing the student to earn credit while working with more experienced technologists in a hospital, physician's office, or imaging laboratory. The more clinical experience a candidate has, the better the chances of finding a good job.

Certification and Licensing

Although certification is not required by law, many insurance providers only pay for sonographic diagnostic procedures performed by certified personnel. Since insurance payments make up the bulk of health care income, most employers require sonographers to be certified. Sonographers can gain certification by completing an accredited program and passing an exam. In addition to educational institutions, certification is available through the ARDMS, a body whose credentialing is widely accepted.

To ensure patient safety, many hospitals and physicians' offices require sonographers to be certified in basic life support, which shows they are trained to provide cardiopulmonary resuscitation, a lifesaving technique commonly known as CPR.

Twelve states require any technician who has contact with patients to be licensed. Licensing requirements vary from state to state.

Volunteer Work and Internships

High school students interested in becoming a diagnostic sonographer should apply for internships at hospitals or clinics. Any position in a hospital or clinic will help the student decide if the environment, including working with patients, suits their interests and personality.

Almost every formal education program for diagnostic medical sonographers includes clinical internships that students must complete before graduating. Students generally are encouraged to complete internships in several settings and specialties so they can figure out in which area of sonography they are most interested.

Skills and Personality

Diagnostic sonography combines a variety of skills—mental, physical, interpersonal, and technical. Diagnostic sonographers must enjoy operating complex machinery and feel comfortable using computerized instruments. They must be detail oriented, able to both follow the testing instructions precisely and to carefully observe and analyze the images on the screen as they conduct the examination.

The sonographer needs excellent hand-eye coordination to move the equipment on the patient's body in a way that captures high-quality diagnostic images. This includes reacting quickly and precisely to the image on the screen and positioning equipment in the right place and at the right angle to record diagnostic attributes of a patient. In addition, diagnostic sonographers must have the physical stamina to spend long periods on their feet. They also need the physical strength to lift and move patients who need assistance.

A sonographer works closely with patients, actually touching them with equipment. As a result, the sonographer must have excellent interpersonal skills to gain the patient's trust and cooperation. This can be especially difficult when the patient is in pain or experiencing mental anxiety about their condition. "Patients really appreciate it when you take a few minutes to explain the anatomy and functions of their organs," says Thorup. She adds:

I'll ask patients, "Have you ever seen your organs before?" Most answer that they have never seen them and don't know much about how the organs silently work every day to keep them healthy. I love taking a few moments to give the patient a "tour" of their organs. Most patients have only briefly learned about human anatomy while in high school, and they are in awe of what they see. Making connections for them in this way is priceless. These types of conversations usually lift their spirits, give them hope, and build their confidence in your abilities.

On the Job

Employers

According to the Bureau of Labor Statistics (BLS), diagnostic medical sonographers held about 60,700 jobs in 2014. The overwhelming majority—68 percent—worked in public and private hospitals. About 20 percent worked in physicians' offices, and less than 10 percent worked in medical and diagnostic laboratories.

Working Conditions

Diagnostic sonographers work inside—usually in rooms set up for diagnostics but sometimes at patients' bedsides. Diagnostic rooms usually are dimly lit or darkened during the examination, so the sonographer can better see the images on the screen. Most sonographers work regular full-time hours, but those who work in hospitals may work evenings, weekends, or overnight, since hospitals are always open and patients can arrive at all hours of the day or night.

Earnings

The salaries of diagnostic medical sonographers vary greatly, depending on experience and geographical location. According to the BLS, the lowest-paid 10 percent of sonographers earned a median annual salary of less than $48,720 in May 2015, while the highest-paid 10 percent earned a median salary about double that amount: $97,390. The median annual wage for all diagnostic medical sonographers was $68,970.

Opportunities for Advancement

While sonographers can increase their pay by continuing their education and gaining certifications, the only opportunities for advancement within a clinical setting are in management and administration. With three or more years of experience, a sonographer might become a lead sonographer or the director of an ultrasound department.

With the required education and credentials, sonographers can move into education, teaching the next generation of ultrasound technicians at colleges, universities, technical schools, and hospitals. Although the starting pay might be lower than that of clinical positions, educators enjoy excellent benefits and job security.

What Is the Future Outlook for Diagnostic Medical Sonographers?

The job outlook for diagnostic medical sonographers is extremely good. Since imaging technology is less invasive, safer, and less expensive than other diagnostic procedures, the private and public insurers that pay for health care encourage the use of this technology to save on costs. In addition, as the baby-boomer population ages, more people will require diagnosis of medical conditions that are common in old age.

According to the BLS, the number of diagnostic medical sonographer positions in the United States is expected to increase from 60,700 in 2014 to more than 76,700 in 2024, a growth rate of 26 percent. That is almost four times faster than the average for all occupations (7 percent). It is also 4 percent faster than the growth of similar positions, such as cardiovascular technologists and technicians, which are expected to grow 22 percent over the same period.

Find Out More

American Institute of Ultrasound in Medicine (AIUM)
14750 Sweitzer Ln.
Laurel, MD 20707
website: www.aium.org

The AIUM is a multidisciplinary medical association of more than nine thousand physicians, sonographers, scientists, students, and other health care providers. Established more than fifty years ago, the AIUM is dedicated to advancing the safe and effective use of ultrasound in medicine through professional and public education, research, development of guidelines, and accreditation.

American Registry for Diagnostic Medical Sonography (ARDMS)
1401 Rockville Pike
Rockville, MD 20852
website: www.ardms.org

The ARDMS administers examinations and awards certification in various areas of ultrasound, including abdomen, breast, musculoskeletal, obstetrics and gynecology, and pediatrics. The website offers career guidance for students and information for educators and patients.

Society of Diagnostic Medical Sonography (SDMS)
2745 Dallas Pkwy.
Plano, TX 75093
website: www.sdms.org

With more than twenty-eight thousand members, the SDMS is the largest association of sonographers and sonography students in the world. The SDMS promotes, advances, and educates its members and the medical community in the science of diagnostic medical sonography.

World Federation for Ultrasound in Medicine and Biology (WFUMB)
14750 Sweitzer Ln.
Laurel, MD 20707
website: www.wfumb.org

The WFUMB is dedicated to the advancement of ultrasound by encouraging research, promoting international cooperation, disseminating scientific information, and improving communication and understanding in the world community using ultrasound in medicine and biology.

Bioinformatician

Bioinformaticians use computers and computational techniques to store, retrieve, organize, and analyze large amounts of biological information. They use this information to learn more about the causes of diseases and to search for treatments for medical conditions. Bioinformaticians do not work with biological samples, such as blood, tissue, or cultures. Rather, they work with the data output of machines that analyze such samples. The field of bioinformatics is considered interdisciplinary because it combines several disciplines to analyze and interpret the biological information: biology, including biochemistry or genetics; mathematics, including statistics or physics; and computing, including software development or data mining.

The need for bioinformatics arose in part from the explosion of publicly available information resulting from the Human Genome Project, which completed the mapping of the 3.3 billion chemical units in the human genetic instruction set in 2003. The genome data is so vast, it can only be analyzed using

At a Glance:
Bioinformatician

Minimum Educational Requirements
PhD

Personal Qualities
Analytical; detail oriented; persistent

Certification and Licensing
Required in some countries

Working Conditions
Indoors

Salary Range
About $42,000 to $113,000 *

Number of Jobs
As of 2014, about 108,000 *

Future Job Outlook
Growth rate of 8 percent through 2024 *

* Numbers are for all medical scientists, a group that includes bioinformaticians

computers. The process of exploring the human genome for medical purposes is known as genomics. Bioinformaticians and scientists in this field use high-throughput equipment to compare sections of the human genome taken from both healthy and diseased volunteers, looking for genetic differences that might cause a disease or help it to spread in some individuals.

In addition to analyzing genes, bioinformaticians use computational techniques to analyze the information associated with biomolecules, such as proteins (in a field known as proteomics) and metabolites (in a field known as metabolomics). Bioinformaticians working in proteomics and metabolomics study how biomolecules interact within the cells to perform complex functions. This is information that can be used to create new targets for drugs and other therapies.

Bioinformaticians analyze much more than publicly available data from the Human Genome Project and other sources. Many design their own experiments or collaborate with other scientists whose experiments have yielded large amounts of data. Bioinformaticians then analyze the data or create models of how the complex systems work. "Biologists have become really good at generating data," Ryan Brinkman, a bioinformatics expert, told the BioTeach website. He added:

> Biology has grown beyond . . . sticking pins into [butterflies] and placing them into a glass case stage. Now we sequence that butterfly's genome and put that data on the web for everyone to download. But once we have our huge pile of information (like DNA sequence), we need people who can put that butterfly sequence into a database, do the analysis, and also put the raw data on the web so other biologists can also have access to it. Of course every biologist who wants that data probably needs to have at least a bit of bioinformatics experience before they can make much use of it. With all the data, you get more interesting ideas of research questions to ask, but since all that data is probably too much to go through by hand, you need to know computers at every stage of the game.

Not all bioinformaticians are scientists who perform experiments or analyze data. Working as part of a bioinformatics team, some bioinformaticians use their background in computer science to design and develop the algorithms, software, or database systems that scientists use to perform data analysis. Other bioinformaticians use their knowledge of computing and biology to serve as liaisons between the scientists seeking to test a hypothesis and the software engineers who create the algorithms and write the software programs that allow the experiment to be carried out.

Scientists working in genomics, proteomics, and other high-throughput biological experimental systems are generating vast quantities of data that may hold the secrets to how certain diseases develop and how they can be stopped. As a result, many universities, government-run laboratories, and pharmaceutical firms have formed teams of bioinformaticians to sift through the mountains of data, looking for nuggets of meaningful biological information. For example, in 2015 the US government launched the Precision Medicine Initiative (PMI), a research program that allocates $130 million to the National Institutes of Health (NIH) to collect genetic and health data from 1 million US participants for high-throughput analysis and $70 million to the National Cancer Institute to lead efforts in cancer genomics. "The PMI will enable a new era of medicine in which researchers, providers and patients work together to develop individualized care," states the NIH website. Bioinformaticians will be essential to the success of this program.

How Do You Become a Bioinformatician?

Education

Bioinformaticians need a PhD to work in research and development positions. Most PhD holders in bioinformatics obtained bachelor's degrees in computational biology or a related field, such as biology or computer science. High school students interested in bioinformatics can prepare for college by taking classes related to the natural sciences as well as math and computer science.

Students in bachelor's degree programs typically take courses in mathematics and computer science in addition to courses in the biological sciences. A firm grasp of statistics and the ability to write software code are essential for bioinformaticians. Most bachelor's degree programs in biology include laboratory coursework. Laboratory experience is vital for a bioinformatician. Students can gain additional laboratory experience through internships with academic laboratories as well as pharmaceutical and medicine manufacturers.

Certification and Licensing

Bioinformaticians are not required to be licensed in the United States, although some foreign governments, such as in the United Kingdom, require licensing to receive government funding. Although most bioinformaticians have doctoral degrees in bioinformatics or computational biology, those with medical degrees or other degrees in life sciences can obtain certification in bioinformatics. For example, Harvard University offers graduate certification in bioinformatics composed of four required courses that take an average of eighteen months to complete.

Volunteer Work and Internships

Bioinformaticians require access to high-powered computers or computing networks to analyze, evaluate, and model large data sets. As a result, few nonprofit organizations have the financial resources to engage in bioinformatics research. However, some existing laboratories operating on tight budgets sometimes allow recent graduates to volunteer as postdoctoral researchers. "Try speculatively applying for work experience opportunities as these are often not advertised," advises Prospects, an online employment agency based in the United Kingdom, on its website. "Employers are sometimes willing to take on volunteers and may allow individuals to work-shadow or even just speak to members of staff working within the profession."

Dozens of colleges, universities, and research hospitals offer internships in the field of bioinformatics, computational biology, genomics, and proteomics. Most of these positions pay, and many include travel, housing, and food allowances. For example, the Johns Hopkins University Center for Computational Biology (CCB) offers a ten-week program for college students and a six-week program for high school students during the summer. "The CCB internship program will provide you with hands-on research experience as part of ongoing projects supervised by faculty in the Departments of Biomedical Engineering, Computer Science, Biostatistics, and Biology, and in the McKusick-Nathans Institute of Genetic Medicine at Hopkins," states the Johns Hopkins website. "Current areas of research include analysis of high-throughput DNA sequence data, analysis of RNA sequencing experiments, studies of the human microbiome, assembly of whole-genome shotgun data from various species, and the development of new computational and statistical methods for genome analysis problems."

Skills and Personality

A bioinformatician combines the knowledge of a biological researcher with the skills of a computer scientist. Bioinformaticians must have advanced mathematics skills because their work often involves the use of statistics to analyze and interpret biological data. While some biomedical software exists, most bioinformaticians design their own algorithms and programs to conduct their research. They must be highly analytical and at the same time be a creative problem solver, able to think of new ways to look at data to better understand medical phenomena. They must be persistent, able to overcome failures and obstacles.

On the Job

Employers

Most bioinformaticians work in college, university, and government laboratories, performing basic research that advances scientific knowledge about how human biological systems work but does not necessarily lead directly to medical treatments. Compared to other research techniques, such as gene splicing, protein structuring, and other physical and chemical experimentation, bioinformatics is relatively inexpensive to conduct. All that is required is sufficient computing power and electricity to run and cool the servers used in research. As a result, some small drug companies hire bioinformaticians, hoping to use publicly available information to identify genetic or other causes of disease that could then be treated with drugs or gene therapy.

Working Conditions

Bioinformaticians work indoors in an office, spending much of their time on one or more computers. Occasionally they meet with their postdocs, collaborators, and principal investigators. The vast majority of their time is spent keeping current with the literature, designing experiments, and running them on high-speed computers. Some time is spent writing, describing the results of their work in research papers. Typically, bioinformaticians set their own hours, which usually exceed forty hours a week.

Earnings

According to Sokanu.com, bioinformatics scientists earned a median salary of $75,150 in 2015. Salaries in this profession vary depending on several factors, including years of experience and the location of the employers. The starting median salary of bioinformatics scientists is about $42,000 per year, while experienced bioinformatics scientists will earn a median annual salary of $112,820. The Bureau of Labor Statistics (BLS) includes bioinformatics scientists among all medical scientists, who earned a median salary of $82,240 in May 2015.

Opportunities for Advancement

The career path for a bioinformatician is identical to that of a traditional medical scientist. After obtaining a PhD, a bioinformatician will first work as a postdoctoral researcher, or postdoc. After coauthoring a number of papers with a supervising scientist, the postdoc can be hired as a full-fledged scientist. Further publication will enable the scientist to move up to senior scientist. A senior scientist with a great deal of experience and a high h-index might become a group leader or principal investigator, overseeing a group of scientists. A group leader might become a chief scientist or director of a laboratory.

What Is the Future Outlook for Bioinformaticians?

According to the BLS, employment of bioinformaticians is projected to grow 8 percent from 2014 to 2024, a little faster than the average for all occupations. As the American population ages, more bioinformaticians will be needed to conduct basic research that increases scientific knowledge and leads to therapies that prevent or treat medical conditions. For example, bioinformaticians will be needed to conduct genetic research and to develop new medicines and treatments used to fight genetic disorders and diseases such as cancer.

A large portion of basic research in bioinformatics is funded by the federal government through the NIH and the National Science Foundation. As a result, federal budgetary decisions will have a large impact on job prospects in basic research: The less funding available, the fewer jobs there will be.

Find Out More

American Society of Human Genetics (ASHG)
9650 Rockville Pike
Bethesda, MD 20814
website: www.ashg.org

Founded in 1948, the ASHG has nearly eight thousand members worldwide, including researchers, academicians, clinicians, laboratory practice professionals, and others who have an interest in the field of human genetics. The society publishes the *American Journal of Human Genetics*. Its website includes a news clips archive, webcasts, and videos.

Federation of American Societies for Experimental Biology (FASEB)
9650 Rockville Pike
Bethesda, MD 20814
website: www.faseb.org

Founded in 1912, the FASEB is the nation's largest coalition of biomedical researchers, representing thirty scientific societies and more than 125,000 researchers from around the world. The website offers "Resources for the Public," including two free publications: *Breakthroughs in Bioscience* and *Horizons in Bioscience*. It also includes a wealth of informative policy statements.

Human Genome Organisation (HUGO)
Graduate Building #101
Ewha Womans University
52 Ewhayeodae-gil, Seodaemun-gu
Seoul, South Korea 03760
website: www.hugo-international.org

Founded in 1988, HUGO promotes the international collaborative effort to investigate the nature, structure, function, and interaction of the genes, genomic elements, and genomes of humans and relevant organisms. For each known human gene, HUGO approves a unique gene name and symbol, which are stored in a database at www.genenames.org. The organization publishes *HUGO Journal*.

International Society for Computational Biology (ISCB)
9650 Rockville Pike
Bethesda, MD 20814
website: www.iscb.org

The ISCB is an international nonprofit organization whose members come from the global bioinformatics and computational biology communities. The ISCB serves its members by providing meetings, publications, and reports on methods and tools; by disseminating key information about bioinformatics resources and relevant news from related fields; and by actively facilitating training, education, employment, career development, and networking.

Medical Laboratory Technologist

What Does a Medical Laboratory Technologist Do?

At a Glance:

Medical Laboratory Technologist

Minimum Educational Requirements

Bachelor's degree or equivalent

Personal Qualities

Detail oriented; good communication skills; physical dexterity

Certification and Licensing

Licensing required in twelve states when working with patients or patient samples

Working Conditions

Indoors

Salary Range

About $41,500 to $84,000

Number of Jobs

As of 2014, about 328,000

Future Job Outlook

Growth rate of about 16 percent through 2024

Medical laboratory technologists use high-tech laboratory equipment to perform scientific tests on human tissue and bodily fluids, such as blood, urine, and saliva. Tests might include cross-matching blood for transfusions or transplants, performing a cell count, chemically analyzing blood or urine for toxic components, or looking for microorganisms, such as bacteria or parasites.

The term medical laboratory technologist normally refers to laboratory workers who hold at least a bachelor's degree in laboratory science or another of the life sciences. The term medical laboratory technician usually denotes a laboratory worker who holds an associate's degree or has received certification training only. Technologists, sometimes called medical laboratory scientists, perform more complex laboratory tests than technicians do. For example, technologists often perform sophisticated manual tests on biological specimens, while technicians may perform more routine tests using automated equipment. Technicians typically are supervised by technologists or laboratory managers. Both types of laboratory workers carry out tests ordered by physicians and other health care personnel.

The vast majority of medical laboratory technicians and technologists work in hospitals and independent medical laboratories, where patients are sent to give samples for specific tests. Medical laboratory technicians and technologists calibrate and operate sophisticated equipment, such as microscopes, cell counters, and computerized instruments in order to perform several tests at once. They prepare tissue cultures for testing, monitor the cultures, keep accurate records of the test procedures and results, and enter results into a patient's medical record.

Technologists working in small laboratories often perform many different kinds of tests, but those working in larger facilities may specialize in one area of testing. Specialists in blood bank technology perform routine and specialized tests to identify blood types and antibodies, testing blood for viruses that might be transmitted during transfusion, and investigate harmful responses of the body to blood transfusion. Clinical chemistry technologists analyze the chemical contents of bodily fluids. Cytotechnologists use a microscope to examine human cells for any indication that a cell is abnormal or diseased. For example, a cytotechnologist might look for cancerous or precancerous lesions, infectious agents, or inflammatory processes. Immunology technologists examine the human immune system and its response to foreign bodies. Microbiology technologists examine blood and tissues to detect the presence of bacteria and other microorganisms. Molecular biology technologists perform complex protein and nucleic acid tests on cell samples.

Medical laboratory technicians also may specialize in one area. For example, histotechnicians cut and stain tissue specimens for pathologists, who study diseases at the microscopic level.

How Do You Become a Medical Laboratory Technologist?

Education

Medical laboratory technician and technologist positions have different responsibilities and require different education. Some medical laboratory technicians enter the field after completing a one-year certification program offered at a hospital. Others qualify by completing a certificate program at a vocational school or in the armed forces. Often a medical laboratory technician will obtain an associate's degree in clinical laboratory science, which not only addresses the practical aspect of laboratory technology but also provides the theoretical background for the profession.

Medical laboratory technologists need to have an even deeper understanding of the science involved in the work, and they require a bachelor's degree in medical technology, clinical laboratory science, or other life sciences. Students in these programs explore such topics as anatomy, physiology, laboratory management, immunology, clinical microbiology, parasitology, and medical ethics.

Many colleges and universities offer a degree in medical laboratory science via two routes of entry: a "3+1" or a "4+1" route. In the "3+1" route, also known as a university-based program, students complete three years of required life sciences coursework at college or university that is affiliated with a clinical laboratory. During the fourth year, the students complete an internship at an affiliated clinical laboratory, usually in a hospital. Upon successful completion of the clinical internship, the student will receive a bachelor of science degree in medical laboratory science. In a "4+1" route, also known as a hospital-based program, students obtain a bachelor's degree from a college or university that offers the required medical laboratory science courses. During their senior year, the students apply for admission into an accredited hospital-based medical laboratory science program. After graduation, the student completes the clinical internship. After completing either route, students are eligible to take the national Medical Laboratory Scientist (MLS) certification examination offered by the American Society for Clinical Pathology (ASCP) Board of Certification.

Certification and Licensing

Medical laboratory technologists handle not only patients' biological samples but also their private medical records. In addition, the results of tests conducted by medical technologists can be of vital importance to the patients. As the state of Florida puts it on its official legislative website, "Clinical laboratories provide essential services to practitioners of the healing arts by furnishing vital information that is essential to a determination of the nature, cause, and extent of the condition involved. Unreliable and inaccurate reports may cause unnecessary anxiety, suffering, and financial burdens and may even contribute directly to death."

As a result, Florida and eleven other states require medical technologists to be licensed. "The purpose of this [law] . . . is to protect the public health, safety, and welfare of the people of this state from the hazards of improper performance by clinical laboratory personnel," states the Florida legislature. Licensing is available through state boards of occupational licensure or departments of health. Requirements vary from state to state, but they can include proof of a two- or four-year degree, a certain amount of laboratory experience, and passing a written exam.

While certification is not required by all employers, most prefer to hire medical laboratory technologists holding MLS certification or the American Medical Technologists certification. To qualify for taking either exam, applicants must have a bachelor's degree from an accredited program and one year of approved experience or completion of a recognized medical technology internship.

Volunteer Work and Internships

Hospitals and medical laboratories need medical technology interns to run basic tests on blood, urine, and other bodily fluids. To satisfy this need and to help students gain valuable laboratory experience, many colleges have programs that connect students with the laboratories seeking help. For example, Michigan State University has created the Medical Technology Internship Matching Program of Michigan to provide a standardized process for computer matching of eligible clinical laboratory/medical technology students at several schools with hospitals throughout the state. Other states and universities have similar programs.

Skills and Personality

Medical laboratory technologists need to have both mental and physical skills to perform their jobs well. They must have good communication skills to follow written and oral instructions to perform the tests correctly and discuss the test results with physicians. They must understand how to set up and operate high-tech laboratory equipment to get accurate readings and results. They also must be detail oriented so they carry out the tests exactly as needed, making precise observations and completing reports accurately.

Since medical laboratory technologists work with biological samples, hypodermic needles, and precise laboratory instruments, they must have the physical dexterity to handle these tools effectively. Medical laboratory technologists must have the stamina required to spend long periods of time on their feet while collecting samples. They also need the physical strength to occasionally lift or turn patients to collect samples for testing.

On the Job

Employers

Medical laboratory technicians and technologists held about 328,000 jobs in 2014. About half—51 percent—worked in public and private hospitals. Another 18 percent worked in medical and diagnostic laboratories. Ten percent worked in physicians' offices, while 5 percent worked in colleges and universities.

Working Conditions

Most medical laboratory technologists work full time. Since hospitals and medical laboratories are open twenty-four hours a day, medical laboratory technologists may work nights, weekends, or holidays. Typically, those who work in the evening and overnight earn slightly more than those who work during the daytime.

Medical laboratory technologists work with infectious specimens and caustic materials on a daily basis. To protect their own health and to avoid contaminating samples, they wear gloves, protective masks, and goggles, or sometimes an entire cleanroom suit. Medical laboratory technologists also follow strict procedures to minimize risk, which includes sterilizing equipment and sometimes placing their hands inside a biological safety cabinet—an enclosed, ventilated laboratory workspace for safely handling material that is or might be contaminated with pathogens.

Earnings

According to the Bureau of Labor Statistics (BLS), the median annual wage for medical laboratory technologists was $60,520 in May 2015. The highest 10 percent earned more than $84,000 per year, while the lowest 10 percent earned less than $41,500. Those working in hospitals and medical diagnostic laboratories both earned a median annual salary of about $61,000. Those working in physicians' offices earned slightly less—about $57,500. Those working in colleges and universities earned a median annual salary of about $54,400.

Opportunities for Advancement

Graduates certified in medical laboratory technology sometimes start out their careers as medical laboratory technicians. With additional training, experience, and certification, a technician can become a medical laboratory technologist. With additional education, experience, or certification, technologists can go on to specialize in one area of laboratory science, such as immunology, histotechnology, or clinical chemistry. Some medical laboratory technologists are referred to as medical laboratory scientists.

What Is the Future Outlook for Medical Laboratory Technologists?

The employment outlook for medical laboratory technicians and technologists is exceptionally good. The BLS estimates the number of positions will grow from 328,000 to 380,000 between 2014 and 2024, a growth rate of 16 percent for the period, which is more than double the rate forecast for all occupations (7 percent).

As with the growth of other medical technology occupations, the increasing age of the American population is a major factor fueling the growth of medical laboratory technologist positions. According to the Pew Research Center, ten thousand members of the baby-boomer generation turn sixty-five years old each day, a rate that will continue for the next fourteen years. By 2030, 18 percent of the US population will be more than sixty-five years old. This aging population will require significantly more medical tests and diagnoses for diseases such as cancer or type 2 diabetes than the present population does. The growing number of tests will require more technicians and technologists to perform them. In addition, more advanced techniques are making all testing more common, leading to a further increase in laboratory procedures. The growing number of tests will require more technicians and technologists to perform them, leading to an increased demand for medical laboratory technologists and technicians to use and maintain diagnostic equipment.

Find Out More

American Medical Technologists (AMT)
10700 W. Higgins Rd., Suite 150
Rosemont, IL 60018
website: www.americanmedtech.org

Founded in 1939, the AMT is a nationally and internationally recognized certification agency for a range of medical professionals, including medical technologists and medical laboratory technicians. The AMT is accredited by the National Commission for Certifying Agencies for all its competency-based examinations.

American Society for Clinical Laboratory Science (ASCLS)
1861 International Dr., Suite 200
McLean, VA 22102
website: www.ascls.org

The ASCLS is a national professional society dedicated to establishing, developing, and maintaining the highest standards in clinical laboratory methods and research. It publishes *Clinical Laboratory Science*, a quarterly scientific journal, and *ASCLS News*, a monthly newspaper. The website offers education and career information, including webcasts and podcasts.

Association for the Advancement of Medical Instrumentation (AAMI)
4301 N. Fairfax Dr., Suite 301
Arlington, VA 22203
website: www.aami.org

Founded in 1967, the AAMI is a nonprofit organization dedicated to the development, management, and use of safe and effective health care technology. The organization provides its seven thousand members with courses, conferences, and continuing education, including certification programs. It publishes a weekly online newsletter, a monthly newsletter, and a peer-reviewed journal published six times each year.

Association of Medical Laboratory Immunologists (AMLI)
website: www.amli.org

The AMLI was organized in 1987 to bring together professional and technical people engaged in the practice and study of medical laboratory immunology. The organization consists of clinical scientists, physicians, medical technologists, and other professionals engaged in all areas of current laboratory testing. The website includes educational resources, a job board, and more.

Interview with a Medical Research Scientist

Prasanna Kolatkar is a senior scientist at Qatar Biomedical Research Institute, Hamid bin Khalifa University in Doha, Qatar. He has worked as a biomedical scientist for twenty-five years. He answered questions about his career by e-mail.

Q: Why did you become a medical research scientist?

A: I was always interested in knowing what's behind any black box. Regardless of topic, I always wanted to know what makes something tick. I was especially interested in human health issues and what keeps us healthy. It's amazing how complex all organisms are, regardless of size, and of course human beings are at the apex of complexity, especially when factoring in the greater role of the mind in human interactions. What is interesting is that the genetic differences between humans and many other organisms are very small. This has been quite a puzzle for a long period of time, but modern high-throughput genomic methods that analyze genes of different organisms are showing how nature can make slight modifications that completely change how the same genetic information is read out. My own work involves understanding proteins and DNA at the atomic level using X-ray crystallography (which is a like an extremely powerful camera).

Q: Can you describe your typical workday?

A: My typical workday consists of many parts, including working in the office and the laboratory. The office is the most important part for me, because I am a principal investigator and thus must plan

74

new investigative directions and the ensuing experiments. This is the most critical part for any laboratory, as the game plan is the fundamental driving force for anything—from sports to science. I have to constantly think about what constitutes the most relevant questions that need to be answered. Once the questions are composed, I need to think of the relevant experiments and which teams to form for executing the strategy. The final part is actual experiments in the laboratory that I occasionally have to supervise and help troubleshoot. The primary work in the laboratory is done by students, post-doctoral scientists, and technicians, but I need to keep track of it in case any major errors are being introduced.

Q: What do you like most and least about your job?

A: The thing I like least about my job is that it is impossible to plan when an experiment or project will be finished. You cannot set a certain date. This makes science very different from manufacturing and other engineering fields, as well as other administrative disciplines. Science is not an area that can be predicted or completely planned. In fact, some of the biggest discoveries have occurred as accidents or unintended results.

The thing I most like about my job is the same thing I listed as a problem: It is unpredictable. The beauty of science is that you are uncovering something that no one has previously done. We are constantly making discoveries, and almost any information is new and previously unknown. My work has led to a better understanding of how we get colds, as I was one of the first people to study how common cold viruses hijack a normal human protein for entry into the cell. Other work I have done helped to show how a mushroom protein might enhance our immune systems. The current work I am doing shows how subtle differences in our proteins direct stem cells to completely different outcomes, such as forming neural cells or gut cells.

Q: What personal qualities do you find most valuable for this type of work?

A: The key qualities for any scientist are patience and perseverance. This is one of the most unpredictable areas to work in. It is important to have these qualities so one does not give up at the first failure or "seeming" failure. Science is a marathon, not a sprint. Other qualities include absolute dedication and deep interest. A scientist never stops thinking about his or her work. The ideas are much more important than just the hands-on part. A scientist is constantly thinking about problems and how to best address them.

Q: What advice do you have for students who might be interested in this career?

A: Don't even think about entering this career unless you are deeply passionate about the questions in biotechnology. It is a highly competitive and demanding field where only the most dedicated survive. In addition, be prepared for a long haul, as nothing happens overnight or even in months. It usually takes a few years to have a meaningful result and a story to tell to other scientists or the general population.

Other Jobs in Medical Technology

Biochemist
Biological Scientist
Biophysicist
Cardiovascular Technologist
Chemist
Dispensing Optician
Dosimetrist
Emergency Medical Technician
Epidemiologists
Health Information Technician
Laboratory Animal Caretaker
Life Scientist
Magnetic Resonance Imaging
   Technologist
Materials Scientist
Medical Equipment Preparer

Medical Transcriptionist
Microbiologist
Nuclear Medicine Technologist
Nuclear Technician
Nurse Anesthetist
Occupational Therapist
Optometrist
Pharmacist
Pharmacy Technician
Physical Scientist
Radiologic Technologist
Respiratory Therapist
Statistician
Surgical Technologist
Veterinary Technologist

Editor's Note: The US Department of Labor's Bureau of Labor Statistics provides information about hundreds of occupations. The agency's *Occupational Outlook Handbook* describes what these jobs entail, the work environment, education and skill requirements, pay, future outlook, and more. The *Occupational Outlook Handbook* may be accessed online at www.bls.gov/ooh.

Index